WORLD SOCCER CLUBS

MANCHESTER CITY

by David J. Clarke

Copyright © 2025 by Press Room Editions. All rights reserved. No part of this book may be used or reproduced in any manner whatsoever, including internet usage, without written permission from the copyright owner, except in the case of brief quotations embodied in critical articles and reviews.

Book design by Kate Liestman
Cover design by Kate Liestman

Photographs ©: Mark Cosgrove/News Images/Sipa USA/AP Images, cover; Chris Brunskill/Fantasista/Getty Images Sport/Getty Images, 5; Alex Grimm/Getty Images Sport/Getty Images, 7; Shaun Botterill/Getty Images Sport/Getty Images, 9, 25; Topical Press Agency/Hulton Archive/Getty Images, 11; Allsport Hulton/Hulton Archive/Getty Images, 13; Cattani/Daily Express/Hulton Archive/Getty Images, 14; Alex Grimm/Bongarts/Getty Images, 17; Matthew Ashton/Corbis Sport/Getty Images, 19; Dave Thompson/EMPPL PA Wire/AP Images, 21; Alex Livesey/Getty Images Sport/Getty Images, 23; Michael Regan/Getty Images Sport/Getty Images, 27; Clive Brunskill/Getty Images Sport/Getty Images, 29

Press Box Books, an imprint of Press Room Editions.

ISBN
978-1-63494-960-6 (library bound)
978-1-63494-974-3 (paperback)
979-8-89469-005-6 (epub)
978-1-63494-988-0 (hosted ebook)

Library of Congress Control Number: 2024940869

Distributed by North Star Editions, Inc.
2297 Waters Drive
Mendota Heights, MN 55120
www.northstareditions.com

Printed in the United States of America
012025

ABOUT THE AUTHOR

David J. Clarke is a freelance sportswriter. Originally from Helena, Montana, he now lives in Savannah, Georgia.

TABLE OF CONTENTS

CHAPTER 1
THE FINAL LEAP 4

CHAPTER 2
THE CITIZENS 10

CHAPTER 3
THE NOISY NEIGHBORS 16

CHAPTER 4
WORLD DOMINATION 22

SUPERSTAR PROFILE
KEVIN DE BRUYNE 28

QUICK STATS 30
GLOSSARY 31
TO LEARN MORE 32
INDEX 32

CHAPTER 1

THE FINAL LEAP

Manchester City's players took the field for the 2023 Champions League final. They were looking to make history. A week earlier, the team had won the FA Cup. That is the top cup competition in England. City had also won the Premier League, England's best soccer league. Winning the Champions League would give

İlkay Gündoğan served as Manchester City's captain for the 2023 Champions League final.

City a treble. That rare feat is when a team wins three major competitions in a single season.

City had been the best team in England for more than a decade. Since 2011, the club had won seven Premier League titles. And it had taken home three FA Cups. Despite its success in England, City had never won the Champions League. The club now had an opportunity to be crowned as the best team in Europe.

Manchester City was facing Italian team Inter Milan in the 2023 final. City boasted stars such as striker Erling Haaland and goalkeeper Ederson. Legendary manager Pep Guardiola coached the team. Almost everyone expected City to win. Those

Ederson (right) made five saves during the 2023 Champions League final.

expectations put a lot of pressure on the team's players.

Inter kept the match tight. The game remained scoreless into the 68th minute. Then City defender Manuel Akanji slid a

7

pass into the Inter penalty area. Winger Bernardo Silva raced onto it. He tried to chip the ball into the center of the box. An Inter defender blocked the cross, though. The ball bounced out to Rodri. The defensive midfielder wasn't known for scoring goals. But he blasted a shot into the net.

THE SAVIOR

Soccer experts consider Ederson to be one of the best goalkeepers in the world. He proved it in the 2023 Champions League final. With two minutes left, Inter forward Romelu Lukaku had an open header from only six yards out. Ederson turned it away on the goal line with his foot. One fan called it the "greatest save in Manchester City history."

Rodri smashes a shot to score the only goal of the 2023 Champions League final.

Inter pushed hard to tie the game. Ederson stepped up to make several key saves. He even punched away an Inter header just before the final whistle. That secured the treble for Manchester City. The win cemented the club as one of the greatest teams in soccer history.

CHAPTER 2

THE CITIZENS

In 1880, Pastor Arthur Connell wanted to help his community. He served in a Manchester neighborhood known as West Gorton. Many of its residents were poor. The area was also violent. Arthur's daughter Anna suggested creating a soccer team. It would give local men something to do. The pair started a club called St. Mark's. The

Before a match in 1924, a fan hands a Manchester City player a replica of the team's mascot.

club's name changed a few times. In 1894, it became Manchester City.

Over the next century, City didn't have much success. The club became known for being inconsistent. City won its first English title in 1937. The next season, it was relegated. No other English team has ever been relegated the season after winning a title. In the 1957–58 season, the Citizens scored 104 goals. But they also gave up 100.

By 1965, City still had only one title to its name. The club was playing in the second division that year. City hired manager Joe Mercer. He quickly turned things around. Mercer put together a team around star midfielders Colin Bell and

Mike Summerbee (left) played 449 games for Manchester City from 1965 to 1975.

Mike Summerbee. Striker Francis Lee led the attack.

By the final day of the 1967–68 season, Mercer's team had a chance to clinch a championship. They just needed one more

Team captain Tony Book lifts the FA Cup after Manchester City's victory in 1969.

win. Summerbee and Lee both scored. Manchester City won 4–3. The club went on to win the FA Cup the next season.

Mercer left the team after the 1971–72 season. For most of the next 30 years,

City went downhill. Even worse, local rival Manchester United became the top team in the country. City hit rock bottom in 1998–99. That season, the club was relegated to England's third division. However, help was on the way. City would soon turn things around.

BLUE MOON

The song "Blue Moon" can be heard at every Manchester City game. A blue moon is when two full moons appear in the same month. The term is used to describe a rare event. In the 1980s, Manchester City rarely won road games. After one road win in 1990, fans who'd traveled to the game started to celebrate. They jokingly sang the song. It quickly became a club anthem.

CHAPTER 3

THE NOISY NEIGHBORS

In 2008, Manchester City went up for sale. A wealthy group from the United Arab Emirates purchased the team. Suddenly, City was one of the richest clubs in the world.

The new owners started putting together a top team. They brought in superstars such as defender Vincent Kompany. He eventually became the

Vincent Kompany captained Manchester City from 2011 to 2019.

club's captain. Midfielder David Silva arrived in 2010. Striker Sergio Agüero joined a year later. These players all became club legends. And they helped City compete with Manchester United. Longtime United manager Alex Ferguson wasn't impressed, though. He dismissed

WELCOME TO MANCHESTER

Manchester City and Manchester United fans love to taunt each other. City fans often point out that United's stadium is not actually located in Manchester. It's in a suburb called Old Trafford. When City signed striker Carlos Tevez from United in 2009, City fans had some fun. They placed a blue billboard of Tevez's face at the entrance to the city. The sign read "Welcome to Manchester."

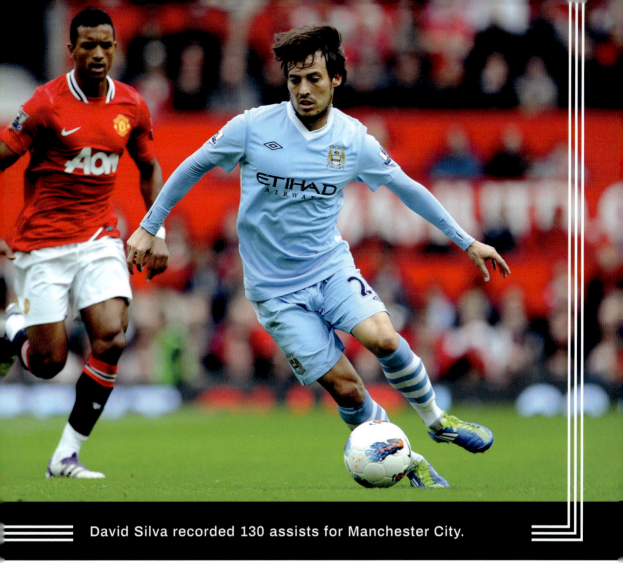

David Silva recorded 130 assists for Manchester City.

City's growth by saying "sometimes neighbors are noisy."

By the 2011–12 season, the neighbors had caught up. City and United entered the final game of the season even in the standings. But Manchester City held the tiebreaker. A win would clinch the title.

The matches were played at the same time. Manchester United finished its game first with a 1–0 win. At that time, City trailed Queens Park Rangers 2–1. The match was in stoppage time. United fans started to celebrate. Meanwhile, fans at City's Etihad Stadium watched nervously. Then striker Eden Džeko tied the game with a header. But City still needed another goal. Moments later, Agüero got the ball. He exchanged passes with teammate Mario Balotelli. Agüero then moved into open space in the penalty area. He smashed the ball from a tight angle. It soared into the back of the net.

Sergio Agüero celebrates after scoring the goal that secured the 2011–12 Premier League title for City.

Agüero ripped off his shirt. Then his teammates mobbed him in celebration. City fans exploded with joy. The noisy neighbors had stolen a championship from their rival. And City was only getting started.

CHAPTER 4
WORLD DOMINATION

Manchester City won the Premier League title in 2013–14. Once again, City clinched the championship on the final day. The club's squad had many stars. Vincent Kompany and goalkeeper Joe Hart formed a strong defense. David Silva and Yaya Touré were two of the league's best

Yaya Touré scored a team-high 20 goals for City during the 2013–14 Premier League season.

midfielders. And striker Sergio Agüero finished off attacks.

However, the team slipped in the standings over the next two seasons. City also struggled in the Champions League. Club owners decided to hire the world's best manager. Pep Guardiola had won many titles in Spain with Barcelona. He had also led Bayern Munich to three straight German league championships. City brought him aboard in 2016.

In Guardiola's first season, City finished third. Then in 2017–18, the club crushed the Premier League. City broke several records. The club won 32 games. It also outscored its opponents by 79 goals. City became the first Premier League team

Pep Guardiola lifts the Premier League trophy in 2018.

to reach 100 points in a season. The second-place team finished with 81.

The next year, City won the Premier League, the FA Cup, and the League Cup. No English team had ever done that before. Even so, the club still had unfinished business in the Champions League.

Some older players moved on. But City signed new stars. Midfielder Kevin De Bruyne became a top playmaker. Attacker Phil Foden came out of Manchester City's academy. Striker Erling Haaland arrived ahead of the 2022–23 season. He scored a record 36 Premier League goals in his first season. That same year, City

FINAL DAY MAGIC

Manchester City pulled off another miracle on the last day of the 2021–22 season. The club needed a win to secure the title. After 75 minutes, City trailed 2–0. The Citizens then scored three times in a five-minute span to claim victory.

Erling Haaland scored 90 goals during his first two seasons with Manchester City.

finally achieved its goal of a Champions League title. The next year, City won its fourth straight Premier League title. No team had ever won four first division English championships in a row. The club had come a long way from its early days. Now City was on top of the world.

SUPERSTAR PROFILE

KEVIN DE BRUYNE

Kevin De Bruyne didn't have blinding speed. He wasn't the biggest, either. His strength was his vision. "He sees absolutely everything," Pep Guardiola once said. De Bruyne always seemed to make the right pass. If none of his teammates were open, he could rip hard, accurate shots from outside the penalty area.

City is a team of star players. The Belgian midfielder might be the most valuable of them all, though. That showed in 2023–24. De Bruyne missed the first half of the season due to an injury. He returned on January 13, 2024. The team began the day in second place.

De Bruyne didn't start the game against Newcastle. In the 69th minute, he came off the bench with his team down 2–1. He recorded a goal and an assist. That lifted City to a 3–2 win. The club didn't lose any Premier League matches from that point on. And at the end of the year, City won its fourth straight Premier League title. The Citizens couldn't have done it without their midfield magician.

In 2022, Kevin De Bruyne recorded his 94th Premier League assist. That broke David Silva's record for most Premier League assists by a City player.

QUICK STATS

MANCHESTER CITY

Founded: 1880

Home stadium: Etihad Stadium

English league titles: 10

European Cup/Champions League titles: 1

FA Cup titles: 7

Key managers:

- Joe Mercer (1965–71): 1 English league title, 1 FA Cup title
- Roberto Mancini (2009–13): 1 Premier League title, 1 FA Cup title
- Pep Guardiola (2016–): 6 Premier League titles, 2 FA Cup titles, 1 Champions League title

Most career appearances: David Silva (436)

Most career goals: Sergio Agüero (260)

Stats are accurate through the 2023–24 season.

GLOSSARY

academy
A program set up by a professional soccer club to develop young players.

assist
A pass that leads directly to a goal.

cross
A pass sent into the penalty area from the side of the field.

penalty area
The 18-yard box in front of the goal where a player is granted a penalty kick if he or she is fouled.

playmaker
A player known for creating scoring chances for his or her teammates.

relegated
Sent down to a lower league after finishing a season with a bad record.

rival
An opposing player or team that brings out the greatest emotion from fans and players.

stoppage time
Time added to the end of a soccer match to account for stoppages in play.

tiebreaker
A system used to decide a winner between two teams with the same record.

TO LEARN MORE

Clarke, David J. *Soccer Strategies*. Minneapolis: Abdo Publishing, 2024.

Hanlon, Luke. *Erling Haaland*. Mendota Heights, MN: Press Box Books, 2025.

McDougall, Chrös. *The Best Rivalries of World Soccer*. Minneapolis: Abdo Publishing, 2024.

MORE INFORMATION

To learn more about Manchester City, go to **pressboxbooks.com/AllAccess**. These links are routinely monitored and updated to provide the most current information available.

INDEX

Agüero, Sergio, 18, 20–21, 24
Akanji, Manuel, 7

Balotelli, Mario, 20
Bell, Colin, 12

Connell, Arthur, 10

De Bruyne, Kevin, 26, 28
Džeko, Eden, 20

Ederson, 6, 8–9

Ferguson, Alex, 18
Foden, Phil, 26

Guardiola, Pep, 6, 24, 28

Haaland, Erling, 6, 26
Hart, Joe, 22

Kompany, Vincent, 16, 22

Lee, Francis, 13–14
Lukaku, Romelu, 8

Mercer, Joe, 12–14

Rodri, 8

Silva, Bernardo, 8
Silva, David, 18, 22
Summerbee, Mike, 13–14

Tevez, Carlos, 18
Touré, Yaya, 22